GOOD
NIGHT
THE
PLEASURE
WAS
OURS

Praise for *The Voice in the Headphones*

"David Grubbs's books are at once bravado poetic performances and incisive works of performance theory. He combines a deep knowing with a willingness to smash everything. I will follow him into any medium."—BEN LERNER

"It's decades now that David Grubbs has kept my head spinning with ideas about the creation, performance, and understanding of music. To hear or read his work is to be invited into collaboration. We are all audience, all of the time, and every creator worth her salt knows this. Grubbs turns this tenet into poetry."
—WILL OLDHAM, music maker

"'Enmesh yourself in a music where it's impossible to take a wrong step.' In that single line, one is reminded of the varied experiments that Grubbs has been part of throughout his career; we see how the studio has been the source of much inspiration, and that deep immersion is what breeds fearlessness."
—JOSHUA MINSOO KIM, *The Wire*

"[*The Voice in the Headphones*] is an experience encapsulated in the space-time of the recording process of isolation booths, mixing boards, the room that not only floats acoustically but also is free from the flow of real time in the outside world.... This is an insider's inside book about an inside experience, but Grubbs' warmth will appeal to anyone who's wondered just what goes on in those sequestered rooms."—GEORGE GRELLA, *New York City Jazz Record*

"Grubbs uses the set-up to extrapolate many philosophical questions surrounding the materiality of technology, the motivations of the performer, the collapsing of distinctions between different media and musing on the economics of entertainment—all within the crucible of the noble ruin of the recording studio, once the promised land for an aspiring musician and now an expensive obsolescence.... A kind of torrent of ideas and anxieties in the form of a visual score pouring forth from his three decades of recording in grungy studios and gilded arts academies all over the world."—ALEX NEILSON, *Record Collector*

Praise for *Now that the audience is assembled*

"David Grubbs's tone poem on the vibratory consciousness betwixt performer and listener rings with an intellect both spiritual and Earth-activist. A sublime sense of provocation is at dance with the O-mind bliss of Kenneth Koch's *The Pleasures of Peace*, Pauline Oliveros's 'The Collective Intelligence of Improvisation,' and Albert Ayler's *Music Is the Healing Force of the Universe*. David's meditation joins hands with these critical, artful signals of love, mercy, hope, and beauty in an enlightened and welcome vision."—THURSTON MOORE

"The three claps are sounded, and all hell breaks loose. In the band, in the orchestra, in the performer, in the gong bath, in the lifting piano, in the audience, in the concert hall, in the venue of the mind. David Grubbs's piece is a noisy page-turning hallucinatory rush."—CAROLINE BERGVALL, author of *Drift*

"*Now that the audience is assembled* . . . reminds us that listening can feel stranger than dreaming."—CHRIS RICHARDS, *Washington Post*

"Primarily, in the beginning, this is a discourse on—and through—rhythm, on what it means to pause and to repeat, on all the many shades of the same and its other, of noise and silence. That the book is able to make you pause and think about all these things while being itself rhythmically (and musically) interesting is no small feat. On top of that, it also manages to be very funny."
—ROBERT BARRY, *The Wire*

"Grubbs's writing does triple duty as a poem, a book, and a score for live performance—like almost all of Cage's writings. . . . The best thing about this book, for me, is that it demonstrates that great scholarship can be great art and that scholarly inquiry on the nature of experimentalism can itself be experimental."
—SARA HAEFELI, *American Music*

"This long form poem is as much a reflection on the contemporary music audience and their responses to an unnamed musician's experimentation as it is a commentary on the act of spontaneous creation. Grubbs's writing style—ephemeral and esoteric, with patches of lucidity and remarkable wit—is highly engaging and entertaining, offering a thoughtful experiment in music writing that invites the reader in to participate themselves, performing as one of the assembled audience."—TOBY YOUNG, *Twentieth-Century Music*

Praise for *Records Ruin the Landscape*

"One of the chief joys of this book is that [it] seeks to rediscover the avant-gardes of the 1960s in all their spontaneity, in their present-ness, as if unfolding these mavericks from their own perspectives, without benefit of current hindsight. We learn, reading this book, what the future looked like to the past. *Records Ruin the Landscape* seeks to prestidigitate the landscape of the 1960s back to life. For this, one should be thankful—including for the recordings that allow David Grubbs' act of imagination and scholarship to have taken place."
—DANIEL HERWITZ, *Critical Inquiry*

"For compositions whose whole raison d'être is to generate a drastically different realization with every performance . . . no recording of any one performance could be said to 'be' the piece. . . . David Grubbs's exhaustively researched *Records Ruin the Landscape* explores this dilemma specifically as it affected the generation of avant-garde composers who hit their stride in the sixties, John Cage being the most prominent and outspoken among them."
—DAVE MANDL, *Los Angeles Review of Books*

"The risk writers run, of course, with the big questions approach, is universalizing their personal narrative in order to present the big answer. Grubbs is too skilled and self-aware to run into this problem. His breadth of research in musicology and aesthetic theory is balanced in this short and engaging book with candid writing about his own experiences of recordings of experimental music. . . . It is testament to Grubbs's sensitivity as a writer that a sympathetic picture emerges of these musicians, who seem often to be railing against hierarchies they can't quite help being part of."—FRANCES MORGAN, *The Wire*

GOOD NIGHT THE PLEASURE WAS OURS

DAVID GRUBBS

DUKE UNIVERSITY PRESS *Durham and London* 2022

© 2022 DUKE UNIVERSITY PRESS
All rights reserved
Designed by Matthew Tauch
Typeset in Garamond Premier Pro and Canela Text
by Copperline Book Services

Library of Congress Cataloging-in-Publication Data
Names: Grubbs, David, [date] author.
Title: Good night the pleasure was ours / David Grubbs. Description: Durham : Duke University Press, 2022.
Identifiers: LCCN 2021039219
ISBN 9781478015543 (hardcover)
ISBN 9781478018179 (paperback)
ISBN 9781478022787 (ebook)
Subjects: LCSH: Musicians—Travel—Poetry. | Concert tours—Poetry. | Music—Performance—Poetry. | LCGFT: Poetry.
Classification: LCC PS3557.R76 G66 2022 |
DDC 811/.54—dc23/eng/20211013
LC record available at https://lccn.loc.gov/2021039219

Cover art: Roger Brown (American, 1941–1997), *Lake Effect*, 1980. Oil on canvas, 72 × 72 in. © The School of the Art Institute of Chicago and the Brown family.

Contents

GOOD NIGHT THE PLEASURE WAS OURS   1

Afterword   151

Acknowledgments   155

Image Credits   158

GOOD
NIGHT
THE
PLEASURE
WAS
OURS

The child persists in speaking a language the adults don't understand. The adults persist in responding in a language the child rejects as gibberish. What this unaccompanied kid is doing at sound check is on her dad, who's out scaring

up catering. It dawns on the child that the musicians don't communicate using words, the three of them flummoxed by the most basic questions. They don't laugh at jokes, they laugh between jokes, they fake-laugh at nothing and nowhere. She starts again and delivers it differently, cascading impatient tones accelerating toward birdsong, still to no effect other than the blankly expectant faces of adults. All of this flickers hilarious and exasperating to the child—she's not giving up—and jibes with her experience of the steady influx of mute visitors carting musical instruments, clinging to, futzing with, sheltering behind.

The daily flow of ridiculous strangers.

Every stage its own stickiness. Stu Sutcliffe

trod these perilously gapped planks of wood, Pete Best did his very when he bashed his kit night after night on this exact spot. Here at the center of medieval St. Pauli pilgrims still alight and descend the narrow wooden staircase to amble onstage and inspect the damage wrought by boots and bass drum spurs. This celebrated stage could pass for a thousand years old; it gives unpredictably with each step during the load-in, each uncertain stagger step beneath an amplifier to be positioned just so, an awesome decades-old pilsner

lacquer postponing inevitable collapse.

After sound check a stroll down one of the narrower streets off Reeperbahn delivers the jet-lagged trio to a bar devoid of graffiti or mosaic

of touring bands' stickers. Sepulchral barroom oxygen. It's hard to picture who favors this abandoned locale and what time they arrive. There's a back room, more like someone's living room, but quieter, darker, uninhabited. Someone's grandparents' or great aunt and uncle's windowless subterranean rec room with stained wood paneling, dusty desiccated couches, and overstuffed armchairs accented by a half dozen framed prints of Prussian military uniforms from 1870. The sole element that suggests late twentieth century is a coin-operated pool table—the trio thankfully provisioned with D-mark coins—and a wall-mounted rack of translucent, bile-colored fiberglass cues. Kill an hour, train yourself

to fix the spot in memory, confirm its existence

down the line with musicians slotted along a similar circuit. Several hours later, in one of the smallest venues of the tour, one of the most deliriously crowded and vilely pitlike pungent, musicians and audience surge back and forth in wavelike motions across a fugitive gap, a lopsided tug-of-war of three versus one hundred with each side blithe to the other's backstory, pleasurable seething siege, smudgeable history painting commemorating Thursday or Friday or Tuesday and whoever rolls into town

whichever town, just a band

just a crowd, but over three-quarters of an hour—some nights it happens within ten seconds—the two sides wake and warm to the excellence of the other. Plumb the mystery of the first encounter with both sides partaking in, demanding volume and group churn. Mandatory eye contact means it's everyone's churn. Overwhelming ricochet superimposes reflection upon reflection

agglomerates, laminates

embosses

sph-

ere bi-

sected by cymbal

shimmer. Amplify everything.

It's easy to learn the thing that makes the audience howl: the pulling up quick, potent milliseconds of silence, tinnitus pre-echo, tremor

graduating to temblor, ominous absence

of impact. Don't leave me bewildered, there's only one thing I can do there's only one thing I can say. We're still waiting, zoomed in disorientingly close, helplessly inhabiting a moment between, a rapidly unspooling string of moments before the next beat arrives. Electricity spreads silently through the atria, through every dramatically stilled chest in the joint. The sharpshooter's calm between beats. Screenshot the trough of a wave take aim, take care to aim with redoubled care amidst abandon and the abandonment of downbeat. In the halted progress of chaos a flying fish seizes midair

Bull's-eye. There's still time to squeeze off a second shot between beats, in the stillness after the catch of a crash cymbal between thumb and forefinger, energy transferred from bronze alloy to drummer's throbbing golden arm. In the multiform stillness that follows the muting of strings, amplifiers at the ready, amplifiers humming, amplifiers pawing and pleading to do what amplifiers do best, always at the behest. Everyone, don't breathe

not yet

continue to hold this call may be, come on this is nothing, the time it takes for eyes to widen comically or batten down in advance of a plunge, a fork in the audience's road of self-preservation. The horizon of the event curves with an abrupt raising of drumsticks and three musicians' telepathic twitch, gravity torques, and down we go. Everyone hold that breath

then scream like we rehearsed

just kidding there was no rehearsal, there's never a rehearsal, just scream everybody because that's how we sound the missing chord, the multiple-octave cluster of however many forearms across the keyboard, knocking the wind out of, disabusing disused pipes. Some go high and some bellow and bray as low as they can, to each their own scream the chord voiced as the occasion demands, and impossible

to improve upon. It's the scream this audience instinctively feels it was
convened to make, the scream this audience was destined to and damn
right deserves to make, the house

screams its collective authority, finds its unifying aesthetic then in a flash is cruelly overmatched.

The musicians see an opening and pounce. They produce a jagged deafening sound, the most lacerating attack of which they're collectively capable. All the howling voices in the room are enveloped, voices recast as unheard music

lungs strain and throats burn to no audible effect, blood vessels in the brain narrowed, silhouettes pitched forward in forceful completion of exhale. The audience ministers to its dizziness with a synchronized slug of Flensburger Pils. Then they take a shared deep breath and scream again. Maybe a hundred against three doesn't seem such a fair fight, not with the band's amplification, the sound caroming like mad and attacking from all sides. The musicians flatter themselves that they're in command of the situation. Over the course of the tour each of the three band members will come to regard this gesture and its response differently, whether as manifestation of daily or nightly improvised community, as physical release, as bulletproof joke

stupider and more profound with each telling, as musicianship, as showmanship, as diagnostic stimulus, as difficult-to-shake habit, as gesture, as empty gesture, as placeholder, as void, as vacuum, as ventriloquy, as puppetry, as political theater, as incoherent political theater, as violence, as carte blanche, as cashed-in chips, as blanket disrespect.

The audience won't lose sleep over it

instead confident that they're the ones who make it happen. The trick is in the timing in which the audience takes understandable pride; the lacerating et cetera roar doesn't arrive until they give the sign, and it's in their power

to leave the band hanging through what could devolve into the unending pickup. The audience might turn tail and march up the steps and out of the venue in protest, past the merch table with neither glance

nor purchase, the bartender and sound engineer and promoter as well, everyone could choose to pack it in and leave the trio alone to end the standoff—the night their bluff was called—and break down their gear and let themselves out. The audience decides when not to scream.

A splinter of the true stage

lodges itself in the heel of the bare-

foot drummer. It nests there for decades,

always. One explanation of how a life unfolds.

In the breather before the next song, the tall bass player who's in it for the hell of it—the childhood friend who three months from now will return to libraries and lecture halls, a mensch among music lifers in the making—takes the opportunity to fetch his smokes from a corduroy shearling jacket, shakes the pack, and up jumps a square. He lifts pack to mouth and flicks a brass Zippo up the side of a pant leg, victoriously

lights, sucks. After a lag of scant seconds, a closed-circuit television delay, everyone reaches for their own smokes. The inchoate collective thought bubble of gratification is punctured by a pointillistic sound field of flicks and match strikes, and a great exhaled tobacco cloud drifts

toward the stage. The bassist screws the lit cigarette upright between headstock and dropped D string and recommits to not cracking his skull on the low-hanging speakers. Looks to the drummer to count us back in.

For the encore the trio swells to a sextet with unanticipated special guests dropping in and having a bash, the welcome interlopers' gig down the street ending early and thus providing a second rhythm section and roadie moonlighting

as shouty improvising singer—we call this one "Trash Compactor Blues," einzweidreivier!—none of whom the trio had previously met, rather encountering these Midwestern demi-legends through anecdote, firsthand testimony, live tapes, xeroxed photos, flyers, speculative fanzine interviews, and owlish singles and EPs. The cross-generational double trio sprawls four-on-the-floor and succeeds through still more punishing volume and runaway momentum, six bodies bouncing off one another on this smallest and most ancient of stages, the living biblical landscape.

Being six men, conversation is limited to onstage thrusting

with the dissident members of the band from down the street hoofing it back to their own gig before the applause dies, before the trio summon the courage to introduce themselves other than through onstage jousting and playacting. The end of the gig coincides with a procession

of DJs and record crates down the stairs of the venue; there's a line out the door that extends into the street and down the block as audiences for the back-to-back events overlap. Businesslike hands snap folding tables into place onstage, and before the first amp has been moved the needle drops on a freshly unsheathed twelve-inch. The trio's post-show elation

sometimes dissipates in the changeover, sometimes continues to bloom. The group mood is unpredictable and hinges on the slightest of details: the perceived temperature of greetings, body language prized for charming opacity, screwball mistranslation and how quickly the DJ gets people onto the dance floor in these moments of maximum confusion, of simultaneous entrances and exits. An urgent question relates to settings on the time machine

are we entering retro mode or can we all agree to hell with this decade, to hell with what preceded it, will the DJ set the controls so that we can abandon this exasperating decade, the sclerotic century, the abdicating millennium? Don't forget that somewhere at this moment the Arkestra is chanting and marching and beating the drums, unison-singing

ten more years 'til the year two thousand.

Tonight the group packs its gear without delay

piles it in the venue's office to be snagged the following noon, and together with the driver who doubles as tour manager—the one who holds the cash—exits the claustrophobic venue, shuffling past sidewalk currywurst vendors on the way to a club known for raging until 8 a.m., 10 a.m., lunchtime, always tunneling into the next day. The identical twin sisters who organize parties there are beloved by the driver for from time to time throwing a bag of speed his way. This comparatively upscale club is several times the size of the venue of the just-completed gig, a cruciform shape with a large black rubberized dance floor in the center, pillars for peering around at the corners, and steep raked seating on one side with rows of bleachers disappearing into the murk.

To the trio's surprise the dance floor clears

after every song; there are at least three different crowds, three different scenes present in roughly equal numbers, and each group takes its turn in a three-song rotation. It starts with a techno or acid house track that's blowing up everywhere this spring, nonstop arm and upper-body movement, footsteps circumscribed and knees pressed together in athletic corkscrewing, energy pulsing within erect bodies, sweat and flesh and scissored tops, chemical drive for nights and days, arms upward and fingers scraping

the beyond. The final beat of the track cues a Shibuya Crossing in miniature, the skillful brushing-past of opposing squads of pedestrians. This next set of dancers making its way to the floor favors a rockish glam getting down, scarves and curls and swoons like Bolan or Bowie on *Top of the Pops*, air-guitar gestures soundtracked by vinyl surface noise signifying well-loved copies of LPs inherited from an older sibling, aunt, or uncle.

Caveman kick drum floor tom shuffle beat

with voluptuous stereo delay on the voices, at times slathered on the entire mix, football chants ponging from pillar to pole. Two choruses in and everyone on the dance floor is singing along, can't help it, the trio and the driver can't help it, everyone succumbs to Sam

got to be Sam, suave-maned man with telegram

of self-evident significance. The vampires on the bleachers sing along with understatement, the intoning black mass of them. Take a walk in the park at dusk and you might spy a bat, several, then you notice there are dozens, the trees full of them, not a vacant branch, hundreds of silently ripened creatures, patient goths until they're playing their song, at which point hell-bent they rush the dance floor, a wild impatient scramble to replace the glam rockers with capes flying and the odd bared fang. They sprint to the dance floor like Mickey Rivers squeezing out a bunt, the fastest man in the history of Major League Baseball, safe at first and having overrun it by some distance lumbers back to the bag with a beautiful deadpan gait

the slowest walk in the sport. After flying to the dance floor, vampires downshift into lowest gear or idle in neutral, fish out a cigarette and light it to catch their breath, using the glowing tip to draw brokenhearted circles in the air. Three steps forward, a long pause, three steps back, a longer and more grave pause, another wave of the cigarette, smoke because your life

depends on it. Chess pieces agitate for stalemate.

How do the hours pass? With vodkas and bitter lemon, with Cuba libres sweetened by Afri-Cola, with intervening large beers. By avoiding the persistent offer of a lunatic at the bar to join him in a Drecksack—borsa di merda, shitbag—a streaky brown concoction of cola and pastis. The trio chafe congenially

against the three-act rotation on the dance floor, overstaying their welcome and providing unwelcome continuity, feigning ignorance; they're treated as if invisible, especially by vampires whose only acknowledgment of the interlopers is a lowered shoulder and demonstrative low-speed collision. Three steps forward, three steps back, wave cigarette. Who moves

to leave? Anyone except the driver slash tour manager. Never during these six weeks of shows does he mention the lateness or earliness of the hour, the following day's drive, the fact of an early sound check it's unimaginable he'd counsel prudence or be the first to quail. Drink tabs soberingly totaled and by now acclimated to the club's ecosystem of techno, glam, and goth, the trio plus driver ascend the several stairways that bring them to the earth's surface

ambushed by daylight, and how could they have fallen

for it again? Amateurs. This same cataclysmic reveal happened the night before and the night before that, hip-checking or body-blocking panic devices on industrial doors, anticipating darkness and stillness in the dead center of night when instead the city cranked awake hours ago on a Saturday or Sunday or Wednesday. Morning unforgivably bright.

Breakfast coincides with the end of a nearby factory's overnight shift, the only open seats at the counter. Talking means twisting your neck, happens sporadically, then less and less. Eggs, potatoes, toast, sausage, and coffee or beer. Conversation buzzes around them in a language the three musicians understand poorly or not at all, only gleanings from vocabulary words one of them diligently compiles and shares in afternoon puzzlings

across the newspaper's front page, a plan to school oneself in the van. This list of disarticulated parts of speech privileges nouns, doesn't yet meaningfully contribute to conversation, jokes, anything requiring subtlety—only the comedy of arbitrary collection. The growing list of words begs to be reshuffled and drafted for song-lyric duty

poetry crystallized in failed language study

staircase

mountain

to skim

to dampen

to die of thirst

tenderness

intercourse

injured person

suspect

summing up

for the defense

On the television in the café news again arrives from Beijing. The trio access information via satellite images, but also from eyes turned toward the TV screen, dispirited expressions, silence from the wait-

staff and workers. During sound check the day before they had seen footage from a fixed, distant vantage of the solitary protester in white shirt and black pants blocking the advance of tanks on the Avenue of Eternal Peace. The occupation of the square culminated in the army's assault, thousands of green helmets and a bloodied student holding aloft the helmet used to slash his face. Cut to nighttime scenes

of armored vehicles, tear gas, flame-lit video, and the cashier at the end of the counter explains they've shot hundreds, maybe thousands of unarmed protesters. From a mirrored asteroid verdammte Scheisswelt we understood that, cosigned. Rubber legs stagger-carry musicians and driver back to the hotel, bad news regurgitated in stray bitter sentences, ten more years 'til

light on the Elbe, the gray river and the vast port. Light on the dry docks through low cloud cover. Snap a photo of a forty-five-degree slant of light. It travels with you. This image of a beam of light through the clouds terminates in research years later; it haloes a dock emblazoned with the name of shipbuilders synonymous with slave labor.

For now—for then—ignorant gawking.

The airplane is suspended above the ocean for hours by a single cable or very thick rope that at regular intervals is tested by violent turbulence. No one wants to die during rebooted

Batman, block it out. Remove the plastic stethoscope earphones, disengage from the washed-out nighttime chase scene on the distant screen, flip open the overflowing armrest ashtray. Scan for flight attendants to assess their panic level (negligible). Only infrequently does this cable or thick rope break

but when it does the aircraft plummets straight down like an elevator falling for many long minutes. This rare event triggers multiple dream sequences, optical-printed thickets of quotidian imagery growing denser until a single shade predominates, the reigning blot.

Some swear it's more reassuring to imagine the plane hurtling forward at five hundred miles per hour. It doesn't leave much room for error, dodging debris in the troposphere, cotton cloud-

striking. The turbulence and weaving and bobbing could be a good thing if it means that the folks in charge aren't passively accepting their fate, everyone's fate. A friend's story is recalled during each flight, the story of another plane dropping precipitously

after the rope has finally snapped, looking to the flight attendant for reassurance and instead discovering she's hunched over and vomiting, sorry to bring it up. Each passenger a different vision resolving in a different hue. Who can picture the end-credits palette before the alarms sound and oxygen masks burst from their hiding places? Da stürzen die Sauerstoffmasken

aus seinem Hinterhalt. Bring on the turbulence

immediately prior to landing, the rougher the better because we're almost there—one way of demonstrating that you were never actually frightened. Mothball the vow that if we make it to the other side I'll never again cross this ocean, whoever wants to see me can make the journey themselves. Ask me again in six weeks after a next run of shows. Wheels down resets the game.

The Wall was breached the night before, news travels

seemingly not at all if no one wanders past a newsstand or tobacconist. The group, different group this time, take turns carefully stacking instrument cases and hurling duffel bags into the back of the yellow Mercedes van. Rear doors and a sliding door slam shut and the quartet plus driver now plus tour manager head off in search of the ring road and the autobahn that takes them west across the Rhine, leaving the country, headed in the opposite direction of what's unfolding beyond their ken

in the two Berlins. Prepare to surprise punk comrades

taping a television program at noon one country over; it's on the way to the evening's gig and they can spare an hour or two to sit in the studio audience. Their friends in turn will have the pleasure of striking the group dumb by narrating scenes of hundreds of thousands of people crossing into West Berlin on foot or by Trabant, army bulldozers smashing opening after opening, and the imminent resumption of westbound buses. But now everyone has to pipe down

for the television show. First up is the semifamous one, the journeyman songwriter from Southern California who a decade earlier scored a handful of improbable hits. Everyone gives him a wide berth. He strides out stiffly to perform solo, denim and trimmed beard, tinted round glasses and twelve-string guitar, writerly baritone

I want to live in an ivory tower

I want to live like

a smothered cough, nose wiped on his jacket sleeve. Testing, two, three. Attempt to lower the mic stand, wrestle with the mic stand, here comes an assistant speed-walking from the wings to adjust the height of the microphone. Crack a joke irretrievably lost to time

I want to live in an ivory tower

I want to live like

Testing, two, three. Attempt to lower the mic stand still further. Speed-walking assistant from stage right, success. Then an aesthetically satisfying pause to refocus, a sonorous intake of breath, and at the last moment the songwriter decides to raise the microphone a smidge, and the speed walker returns. The songwriter checks the tuning of the twelve-string, makes a cascading series of modifications relative to other tuning modifications with the result that arpeggiated open chords are now less stable than when he began. The twelve-string is rejected in favor of a nearby six-string acoustic guitar. Borrowing a guitar tuner, E A D G B E. Mic stand perfect. Here comes the bookish, darkly striated voice

I want to live in an ivory tower

I want to live like

I'm going to need a short break. Studio-wide exhale, respectful absence of chatter. When the songwriter returns five minutes later, he's removed his jacket and ditched the tinted glasses. Strums a couple of chords on the six-string, decides again in favor of the twelve-string. Needs to borrow the tuner. Coughs, inhales deeply, wipes nose on shirtsleeve. Fixes his attention on the height of the microphone; the speed walker appears, is waved off. The songwriter asks about trying a different mic, and a second speed walker enters from the opposite wing with a selection of three microphones. After a short consultation he makes the swap, here we go, testing, two, three, the voice warmer and deeper still, a genuinely lovely instrument

I want to live in an ivory tower

I want to live like Louis B. Mayer

fetch me the bones of the Elephant Man

paging Garbo, Harper Lee, Miss Havisham

I want to live like Brian Wilson. I beat a retreat

faster than Bobby Fischer. I want to live with a guitar that stays in tune, not a goddamn toy—I need another break. Speed walkers relax. Punk comrade number one leans forward and whispers that the songwriter's boots look uneven, maybe someone needs to sand down the right heel. Hearts go out to the songwriter in his time of implosion, and the audience is left to imagine the form his jabs and feints will take, which names find their place

in the roll call. But everyone's brain is in Berlin

not a doomed television taping and satire in illegible fragments. The songwriter runs out the quartet's clock as the group is forced to leave with the song ever in potential

perhaps still undergoing revision. Back in the van acquired narcolepsy facilitates the daily routine, the quartet asleep before they've reached the next town. Buckle up, tuck in using winter jackets as blankets, rest the head at an economical tilt of ten or fifteen degrees

and sleep comes quickly and reliably. The body organizes itself around the evening's onstage exertion, prepares psyche and soma for sixty minutes of wakefulness unmatched elsewhere in the day. To live in spurts engage daytime mock hibernation and lower the heart rate during long drives. For the musicians it's a single hour of work every day, and even calling it work requires irony. (Another band weighs in: It's not only the easiest job I've ever had

it's the easiest job I've ever heard of anyone having.) There must be a less risible term for rolling into a different town every day, the yellow van following a predetermined route to collect a small, serviceable pile of cash each night

thirty pickup points and you're done. Sometimes the drive involves hairpin mountain roads and steep inclines that demand the passengers' concentration; sometimes you hold your breath through near collisions with buses and streetcars; teamwork might mean, che bordello, commiseration in the act of attempting a rush-hour left-hand turn in front of the Colosseum. More often it's the same cows mistaken for the same cows

and the same sheep and goats and same stretch of highway, it's a wonder they arrive anywhere new, traversing daily this same strip of farmland, or what passes for such when three-quarters asleep, preparing for the mandated hour of onstage letting go that crowns each day. A regular rotation of a limited number of hard rock, punk, and metal mixtapes—driver's choice, he's doing the work—reinforces the sense of one and the same daily vista. Days of the week aren't so important. There's an uptick in attendance starting on Thursday, larger towns and cities barnstormed over the weekend, back to the sticks at the start of others' workweek.

Dream of a fax waiting for you

scroll of semigloss thermal paper with telltale heartrending handwriting that awaits your arrival. We have a fax for so-and-so, pass the baton to the relay's anchor. The tour writes itself as slow epistolary novel

interrupted by the rare international phone call and the calculation of adding or subtracting six hours, living in what's negligibly the future and taking undue pride in productivity before folks at home begin to stir. Which of these codes still work? By the end of the tour, rolls of fax paper have become treasured possessions

scrubbed by touch to where they're almost entirely faded. The van follows the same route as the truck crisscrossing Europe delivering copies of the current underground hit. For weeks upon arrival at each venue the band is feted with the same record, one that's arrived earlier in the day—quick, someone put it on—and it's spun four or five times over the course of the evening, play it before and after the set, play it for the night's final drink while somewhere delivery is being readied for tomorrow's venue.

Stopping for lunch, beware the vanishing drummer

the same uncanny disappearance whenever the group sits down for a midday meal: I'm just gonna stretch my legs. When the meal ends and the check is settled, back to the van—where did he go? Stretching his legs. The group learns to ask if there's a Harley dealership nearby, anyplace that sells motorcycles. There's usually one within walking distance, and they pile back into the yellow Mercedes, scanning for the dealership they've been told is just ahead on the left or the right. Slow down, honk, and slide open the door; the drummer jumps in without a word before the van comes to a halt.

[…]

I just wanted

to let these Austrians know

a brother from California was visiting.

The largest venue of the tour is an empty spacecraft

a new concert hall at a university where what seemed a low ticket price must be a deal breaker. Thirty minutes before set time, one hour after doors have opened, and it could be the middle of the day, could be nine in the morning. It doesn't appear that anything is happening tonight. Thankfully Igor with the briefcase

already paid, the ominous briefcase. The fact that he's ten years older than the average promoter put the quartet on alert. He recommends shopping for leather luggage and other adult activities before taking the group to a bookstore, passing around scrapbooks with surrealist color comics on newsprint pasted in by hand. At ten minutes before set time there's a knock on the dressing-room window the quartet already feeling ridiculous at sequestering themselves in the small dressing room attached to the giant empty venue, when they come face to face

with an audience of one. Someone from the group opens the dressing-room window and in he comes; at first it seems righteous and sweet there'd be a soul brave enough to pound on the window, signal frantically, climb right in

but now people are squeezing through two and three at a time as the line outside starts to grow. Some enter through the window more gracefully than others, several check the fridge and help themselves to a beer before entering the venue, one visitor snags the toe of his boot on the sill and crashes to the floor with a curse amid concerns he's broken his arm. The arrival of the audience through the window shows no signs of abating, and so the quartet starts to serve food that would otherwise go to waste, fruit and bread and cheese and sandwiches and chocolate. Bottles of wine are opened, glasses poured. As the spacecraft on the other side of the door begins to fill, the bottleneck

that is the dressing-room window necessitates a delay in start time. Ten minutes later they're still climbing in, each making the breach and leap in their own style, some with great panache, some chatty and full of questions the quartet can't begin to interpret, some expressionless, some indignant, some cat burglar–like, some wasted. The place had been a graveyard

the gig presumed to be a bust, and the next thing you know it's raging; before the set has begun the men's-room mirror is smashed and someone's freaking out on the bathroom floor. These things do become part of one's associations with a place, justifiably or not.

The border is staffed by guards who refuse to believe the quartet's protestations that the tour is over, that they're only visiting to meet the record label and do some sightseeing while transporting guitars, an electric bass, a bass amplifier and small speaker cabinet on wheels, cymbals and drum hardware, unsold tour T-shirts and LP stock, and a metal toolbox with trace amounts of finely ground glass from a broken amplifier tube

that a border guard sweeps into a folded piece of paper. He returns moments later to announce he's analyzed the sample and determined that it's cocaine, and wouldn't the group like to come clean about their upcoming shows in the UK? The quartet are scandalized

they could pass for such risk-takers, but no

The strip search is designed to humiliate. Thankfully the musicians succeeded in purging every bit of paper documenting the shows scheduled to take place that week in London, even the cherished faxes. A phone call to the record label results in well-rehearsed protestations—they're here for business talks, press, nothing confirmed—and to everyone's surprise the group is waved through

to the final stop of the tour. After weeks of taking it to the stage not only in capitals and commercial centers but also towns, villages, and activist meetups in the countryside, the tour comes to an end in one of the hearts of the industry, meeting after lightly farcical meeting in pub and snooker club, trying to keep a straight face when the discussion turns to managers, publicists, publishing contracts. Years later

what will the scattered members of the group remember of these shows? That what one looks forward to as climax passes like any other night if not less so, the concluding gigs never definitive and over time registering less clearly than a random Tuesday night's typische Jugendzentrum Essen in a suburb of Stuttgart, bubble-letter graffiti even then a decade out of date; or a pack of German shepherds

startling the group after the first chord of the first song causes them to gallop across the stage in a squat in Bern, a former riding school with delicately balanced sculptures of scavenged rusty metal, no we don't want to eat at McDonald's; or 220 volts in the kisser

when accustomed to microphone shocks of 110 stateside, gentle pecks by comparison; or mingled feelings of pride and defeat after blowing the power in a venue, drinks on the house until the electrician who lives up the road can be roused from bed to sort it out; or an end-of-night final check of the dressing room that reveals a horror tableau of rats feasting on the group's pizza—no longer the group's pizza—the same club where one year later the DJ will tell of a rat confusedly trying to escape up the inside of his pant leg or the sight of one of the true progenitors of punk waltzing into the group's sound check only to understand that he was trying to scrounge advance payment on his gig the following night with a pickup band; or a week of shows in which the time-release

activation of a chunk of hash gobbled moments before the start of the set detonates in gloriously extroverted encores, the group shape-shifting before the audience's eyes with only one instance of the bassist taking a step too many

and tumbling off the stage; or a delirious night witnessing a famously saturnine indie group liberated by a minuscule audience so that what begins as a gratuitous, self-mocking encore eventually exceeds the length of the set—with the wildest of hares they play everything they know and a couple of tunes twice—drawing to a close only when the club switches on every light in the house, everyone should play to an empty room once or a magazine photo session hijacked by a dog

ein Mops, a kind of dog for which the group can't summon the word in English, ein Mops named Edgar snorfling with white medicinal powder massaged into the folds of his truncated snout; the photographer thinks it wise to include Edgar in shots with the band, and the one published photo from the session finds Edgar dead center, bulging eyes trained on the viewer, the musicians arranged haphazardly, awkward broad grins and half-shut eyes, little did they know that Edgar was the star of a local television talk show during which the announcer periodically disrupts the dull proceedings by shouting, "Wo ist Edgar?" and the Mops bursts onto the set

the first rule of photo sessions henceforth being

or the ready-made choreography of an opening band's older hired-hand guitarist who arrives three songs into the set, straps on his Les Paul, and performs the Houdini-like feat of removing his winter coat while playing flawlessly, smoking and singing backup and serving as de facto musical director

a shoulder dips and slips out of the coat, a liberated arm

then it hangs diagonally, toga-like, until another shoulder ooches out, wriggles free, never a bum chord in a song constructed of swerves and sudden stops, out comes the entire arm and the jacket falls, held only by the guitar strap until with a limber reach behind the back he yanks it free and lofts it behind the row of amplifiers, nothing amiss, and the graceful completion of his task coincides with the final chord of the song, unconscious effort in all its beauty.

Do these things happen in the metropolis? There's no guarantee that they occur where it's presumed to matter most. The anticipated high note is overwritten by recollections of

the most peripheral killing of mornings, afternoons

an early train up to Micky Sharpz's tattoo parlor in Birmingham with no engravable images in mind, one musician resolving to go with whatever's being inked on the person ahead of him unless it's a pint of lager wearing Doc Martens, which it is. Better to start with the letter A. Afterward—A is for—celebrate with a noontime Guinness before a long throbbing walk back to the train station, retreat to the city that turns your snot black.

Dodge a third day of cold rain as sole viewers

at a daytime screening of a film that crosses a digital threshold with proliferating inserts, competing screens of miniaturized synchrony, Caliban plus calligraphy and countertenors. Take the rest of the day to ponder moviemaking to come

mysterious digital workflow, the brittle opulence.

Those gigs have mostly flown from memory. Chattering voices: We have our own name for him, we call him Cor Whatta, Cor Whatta Drummer! Ticket scalpers for West End musicals and Nirvana, the sounds and sights of a crush of souls in the Edgeware Road tube station and the group's temerity

to bring the bass amplifier on public transportation, lifting and lugging it down flights of stairs, District and Piccadilly to Heathrow for a final escape back to the US only to be reminded that 16:00 and 6:00 in the evening differ crucially. Negotiate to leave the amp with the airline, return in defeat to the city to try again the next day. The presence of smoke

and sounding of alarms in the Earl's Court station prompt a tense evacuation, how many more smoke-filled levels up to the street, well-wishers from earlier in the day will swear to investigators that they sent the vanished group to the airport with instructions and sufficient travel time. Fax the dental records.

When touring the States, go as far west as the Mississippi and then turn for home. Board an airplane if necessary, rent a car and slingshot north from San Diego to Seattle, cross over to Vancouver. Punk rock dungeons visited less frequently

forever merit respect. Reflect on first touring as teenagers with one member of the group not old enough to drive and the senior one needing to be bailed out for stealing typewriters from his high school. Marvel at the sound engineer's candor at their first out-of-town gig, the first words out of his mouth: I been working on my truck all day and don't need your shit.

A decade later the Pacific Ocean no longer an impermeable border.

Did you see outside just now, on the street, look outside. Someone is polishing the pay phone. Just in front of the hotel. Right this instant I'm watching someone take a cloth and spray something into it and scrub the handset of a pay phone.

Different group this time, intergenerational one that's older than some of its members — not members but participants, beneficiaries of a revolving-door policy. Replace tour manager with gallerist moonlighting as promoter, replace driver with two sharply dressed assistants who speak three or more languages fluently. Arriving the night before

the group was chauffeured to a concrete bunker in time to snore through the annual performance by a local dignitary sludge metal trio — gray, brown, black timbres of overdriven amps and whitecap upon whitecap of pooling sound. Wake to the reassuring roar, wake next to a jet engine, observe the cultic forty or so in attendance.

Table tennis jet lag haywire metronome

one fractured rhythm after

the next accelerates

into applause

!

Television coverage of the summer Olympics centers on table tennis, wrestling, and judo. Turn it off to head out into the day, minutes later remember through the fog of existence whatever it is you forgot, carefully retrace steps to the hotel room—the street signs tell you nothing—and what happened to the bed? There was a bed, you were just asleep in it, and now it's vanished. Run palms

along the walls in search of the hidden compartment, confirm that the room is empty save for suitcase and television. Perfect crime. Flip on the table tennis to calm nerves, restart the search. Repeat the process several times, even as the room's not much larger than the bed. The cleaning woman in the hall peers through the open door, senses panic, and points to where the bed has levitated *Exorcist*-style with floor-to-ceiling metal shafts at the four corners. She smilingly, laughingly demonstrates its operation by means of a switch.

You consider crushing yourself beneath it once she's left.

The first-ever Japanese performance by this multigenerational group is an afternoon appearance at a large chain record store in Shibuya. To play for fifteen minutes is all that's required—all that's permitted—and when the group arrives several hundred people are lined up outside. There's confusion about the back line, a small practice amp with two inputs to be shared by three guitarists, no kits for the two drummers, miked messenger bags will have to do. The group remembers they haven't really rehearsed

haven't played in this exact configuration—so much to be done to prepare for the trip—but the ace up their sleeve is a willingness to inhabit real time onstage. The organizers have all but counted them in for the first number

We're ready to go, we're ready are you? The audience is. It's chaotic, a rockier terrain than envisioned, two drummers beating the crap out of their hand luggage, and with meager amplification the whole thing's not louder than a car stereo. The distance the group traveled to deliver this weird approximation

maybe the chaos doesn't matter

maybe chaos is what turns the wheels

and the afternoon audience wouldn't have it any other way—rock with your socks off and pound the hell out of those messenger bags. Four brief songs later the group sits at the head of a receiving line to autograph several decades' worth of albums, hypervigilant fans cognizant of which musician will be permitted to sign which record. The four or five hardiest souls have brought discographies they've personally researched and prepared—dot-matrix printed or gossamer handwritten sheets of tissue-thin graph paper—and they beseech the group to proofread them for errors. Any intelligence on gaps in a discography elicits an apology and a request to write out the missing information.

At a small bar afterward one of the drummers and one of the guitarists struggle to stay awake. The DJ can't help but notice the only Westerners in this intimate setting, with their pile of gig bags and instrument cases and dressed entirely in black. As the needle drops on each new track

the DJ glances meaningfully at them, eager for a response. They're aware of the rudeness of their slumped shoulders and all but resting their heads on the table. A long blink betokens the briefest of naps, they've given up on conversation, and the more inert they become

the more animated the DJ. The musicians must both have fallen asleep only to wake with the DJ inches from their faces, incongruously swaying to an up-tempo fusion showstopper. Without warning he launches into a perfectly synchronized dexterous and demanding air-flute solo, invitation to a duel they're certain to lose.

A monk requires assistance.

Word has reached him that there are native English speakers in the venue, a large theater beneath the Zen Buddhist temple, and he comes downstairs in search of their input on his translation for a conference on peace studies. He's game for all possible teasings out of their suggestions, for anyone to join the conversation, ready to hear the pros and cons of each proposed alteration. Then all is quiet until six

opening acts arrive. The gallerist has concocted a spectacle of ten-minute sets from local performers and a panel of writers and critics, followed by the intergenerational group. Piles of contact-miked metal, homemade percussion instruments, turntables, cases, cables, and mixers are organized into a semicircle of six workstations at the front of the theater, much shaking of hands and bowing and presenting and unwrapping of gifts, all manner of affirmation of shared purpose. The evening delivers

1 sobering dexterity on the decks, two turntables and a sampler forcing the audience to hold their breath between giddy electrical storms, wild shard-shaping to knock notions of virtuosity off-axis

2 silver-haired and black-clad dancer turned percussionist bobbing, feinting, lunging in the darkness with one cymbal, one stick, and periodic unnerving shrieks, irregular stamping, bebop footfall phrases

3 trio of he, she, and giant he engaged in unholy amplified scraping and drumming on rusted springs, alienated labor with shrill unattended feedback appears to pain audience and performer equally

4 youthful postpunk quartet of two gals, two guys, no song over a minute, the counting in striking everyone as more hilarious each time, kids dazzled by their own superpowers, want to buy them a pizza

5 actionist tribute bondage noise performance prompts septuagenarian art critic to rise up in protest, angry outpouring of words for the gallerist, a march up the aisle and slam of the door, one panelist fewer

6 the most desultory of opening acts tosses up a barricade of indifferent jamming until after ninety seconds they stop, declare their set to be finished, and by overwhelming acclaim they're the winners.

The intergenerational group is seated alongside critics in a discussion that never gains traction. The real-time translation that should be used to one's advantage with the gift of time to shape a next phrase—to ride a rhythm of punch lines or subversive under-

statement—founders in gnomic poetry and generalities, this can't be what's being said, this deferential gesturing toward what can't be said can't actually be what's being said, can't be what's not being said and so excruciatingly. At a moment of maximum impasse the gray-haired dancer-percussionist jumps to his feet and brandishes a silver-handled cane

denouncing merchants of bullshit and self-satisfied talkers talking, at least this is what the group understands from the abashed, frowning translators; now he's shaking his cane at and cursing the audience as he becomes the second person of the evening to stomp up the aisle and out of the venue in what resembles the scripted outbursts of professional wrestling. Wait for the next eruption.

Push, pull.

Group push, group pull

eddies within the ensemble, the

count in as a hint of metronome setting

from that point on collective steering of the ship.

Maybe for the audience it glides like a ship, who knows

if not a ship then regatta of homemade boats, rambling river raft race with entrants' crafts ranging from museum-quality reproductions of historic steam ships to sub–Huck Finn snatches of flooring

that instantly sink. A new song means the opportunity to reset the tempo; this simplified flowchart forks faster, slower, or more of the same, and tonight the audience demands faster. Lean into the tempo

too far and the drummers upshift into a thrash beat; pull back precipitously and they halve it and then pare it back to quarter time, entering the realm of rockers downtown.

It hinges on the song.

The group arrives with the advantage of a repertoire drawn from several decades of reconvenings. Every group has its authorizing moment, otherwise no group — none that anyone cares to name. A happy few have multiple such moments, unforeseen opportunities of the wind again at their backs, the chance for a second or third or fourth time to define themselves with and against, simultaneously affirming and opposing, moments that have everything to do with geography and the privilege of being able to pull up stakes and assemble elsewhere a new, timely cast of characters. The repertoire

memorializes alightings

touchings-down in the catalog of songs delivered tonight as hopscotch chronology, spontaneous itinerary with song titles shouted out and the set list scrapped. The doublings-back and long jumps that impressively clear decades, it's all the stuff of footnotes and discographies however lovingly produced

when a phrase lands as never previously. To say this was written

before you were born matters not at all when the song's assembled anew; exigency's the most skillful arranger in the judgment of many wise souls. On this night there's an amiss glory to the occasioning of songs delivered by the patchwork ensemble, the meaning of the material for each performer closely held.

This batch of songs registers as

an unearthing of facts inviting roughness in recitation, songs to endure however they're clad. Songs for which to pass the mic, songs suited to the surprise of who next steps to the fore, who takes their turn to speak or sing or mumble for the group, or from within the group. In the end it does resemble a vessel. In the end monks are certain to have more questions. Tonight we mean it when we say

Good night the pleasure was ours.

Post-show to Shinjuku in a downpour, white-handled clear plastic umbrellas colliding along narrow sidewalks as a large retinue—all the employees of both record label and publicist—lob suggestions for the next destination, a call for karaoke with ice-cream cake and pitchers of beer. The shyest members of the team are invariably the best performers. Before the group has even cracked the phone book–sized binder of songs

a sales rep belts out "My Sharona" as sung by Elvis, followed by a two-woman Japanese tearjerker with well-rehearsed harmonies, everyone packed tightly around a conference table in the tiny eighth-floor room. The visitors' song selections are relentlessly ill-advised—difficult-to-sing showpieces, excessively wordy ballads not recognized by their hosts—resulting in diffident crooning, everyone too polite to express the puzzlement or disappointment they must feel.

The next stop will require skillful negotiation.

The majority of the host party peels off—but only with great and extended fanfare, mock sorrow, unwillingness to be parted—so that the musicians have a chance at entering various seven- and eight-seater bars, behold Maki Asakawa's piano, and after several attempts they receive the green light to squeeze into a cineaste's safe room

a stained-wood vault of booze lit by three tulip lamps, bottles with filmmakers' names penciled on the labels awaiting their owners' return. French is the lingua franca and the proprietress keeps company with a cardboard cartoon cat in a bandit's mask fashioned from a crushed VHS cassette. Whiskey wisely by the bottle. It's unclear how they make it back to the hotel

and the polished pay phones and highlights of the day's table-tennis matches, the bed this time where you left it.

Back in the States, at the start of a show in front of a capacity audience, a singer confidently steps to the microphone and a plastic cup with sixteen ounces of the cheapest beer on tap at this oversized corner bar finds its target

explodes in his face. Different group this time. I think disbelief

is the word. They've been on a months-long upswing, and their homecoming show seemed a celebration until the moment of impact. It's the electric version of an ensemble with no fixed personnel, the former power trio that renamed and rededicated itself, fundamentally altered the mission, sometimes stripping down to two acoustic guitars, twin sketch pads, the whole shebang meant to jibe with public transportation or touring in a compact car, able to occupy a stage plot the size of a couch. Electronic sound reappeared as a medium in which to breathe deeply, for everyone to thrive. Electronic sound returned with resonances mingled, oscillators abetting the sustain of acoustic instruments, overtone-resplendent steel strings otherwise prone to decay and dying, to mortal

transverse shimmer. Participants cast a skeptical eye

on allegiances and needless distinctions between acoustic and electronic; pressure strikes the ear, it fluctuates the microphone's diaphragm, and we grant the engineer permission to measure it forty-four thousand and one hundred times per second. What aids resonance, what facilitates sustain, what may blend, blend what may and o what a whorl! Still, there are sound checks, input lists, dedicated channels. One performs on an instrument or instruments, one acts as an instrumentalist. Take a gig at the neighborhood dive, take a gig at a gallery or jazz club or unfinished space, take the gig

in the parking garage, take most any gig—take them all to manifest a vision of nimbleness and responsiveness to one's surroundings. The earliest outings of a duo version of the group attracted interest in part as novelty, post-postpunk dripping faucet music, the inverse of power

and the obverse of pop. Neglected, not even scorned folk instruments provoked conversation among spectators in the middle of performances while the musicians fantasized about a transparent curtain ringing down at the press of a button the audience sundered by acoustic baffle. They observed friends' bands in the role of oddball opening act in front of vastly larger crowds, three thousand people gabbing over beers, noting that no matter how gentle or ungraspable

however ellipsoidal or ill-suited a song might be for this environment, if it's delivered with a concluding flourish or swell into an unambiguous final attack everyone in the house halts their conversation, swivels toward the stage, and barks

approval, which multiplied by several thousand becomes a triumphal roar. If a piece conversely generates hard-won musical momentum but lands softly in a final decrescendo fifteen hundred conversations resume.

Beyond the reintroduction of electronic sound through the camouflage of acoustic and electronic resonance both roiling and serene, the next wrinkle was to experiment with ripping interjections of noise, malfunctioning punctuation punctuating malfunction, efforts from within to shred the texture of the proceedings, to crash the airplane. Fight or flight

simulator, fricative sizzle of electricity.

The fader's path is straight and true. Scale is a turn of the dial when there's no recognizable source to enlarge, just smug circuitry and engorged transistors, the fictive sound of electricity. Two acoustic guitars in a wipe

dissolve are replaced by a pair of electric organs shoulder to shoulder at center stage, varying only by virtue of the color of their molded plastic casings, a shade of oxygen-rich Vespa red next to Olivetti green gray. The recourse to volume returns, a previously refused depth and dimensionality they had cautiously rebuilt over the last year, the group no longer tasking themselves with always bringing the wrong music.

Hypothesis confirmed: an endless supply of wrong music.

Quietly approaching

quietly receding

Quietly rescinded

one cross-fade

one calendar

year

The homecoming gig begins with stepwise electric organs in waltzing optimistic ascent. A unison makeshift mantra from identical instruments moves out of and back into phase, the composition a memory game of extending and retracting a simple found-object phrase. Hypnosis by seesaw, fort-da fingering

exercises designed to satisfy. The drummer bides his time, handsomely reinforcing the fact of his not playing. This first piece of the evening is a public warming up, essential to remember how good it feels to exercise as part of a team. Everyone stretches, spines elongate for a better view of what's happening onstage; the audience is invited to recalibrate its means of measurement, time passes like so

time passes like sufficiently many

time passes as crossings of a zero point

when the room is full and the musical phrase pronounced slowly and with great clarity, repeated again and again, altered by the movement of time as well as the addition and subtraction and substitution of notes, the shifting of stresses within a phrase as experienced by the quorum. Time passes until the drummer removes his shirt

makes a face like he's leaping out of an airplane, a face like the chute's not opening or he's been given the worst imaginable news about his family, and he responds with an anguished cymbal swell.

The force field that is his pummeling of cymbals cues the organs to conclude their synchronized opening statements. They slow to a halt and swell to peak volume with forearm clusters. Everyone is privy to a unique perspective within this riot of sound—just turn your head—everyone probes the same impossibly thick foliage

in vain. The sound is what your attention grabs, that to which it clings, cognizes: an engine turning over but not catching; several octaves higher voices chattering or chiding or harmonizing with supreme feeling; and in the uppermost register a furious bagpipe moiré making its play for the last bit of oxygen in the room.

Why the metaphors

air

as upper limit, what exceeds sound

object. Fashion a sphere into which sound doesn't leak

,

play

overhead, trace figure eights above

bent staves, chewed stems, viral multiplication of note heads in a cartoon rendering of the gig. The drummer unhooks his jaw

that's a myth, widens his mouth still further, cocks eyebrows, locks eyes with the red organist, turns to make contact with the green-gray organist, back to the red organist, the drummer uncertain which of his bandmates to cue—live onstage triangulation. In the end he closes his eyes, fuck the both of 'em, they're professionals.

They execute a tape edit of a transition too severe to be believed finessing a subsequent splice every sixteen measures when there are measures. Each improbable insert arrives in a different tempo, undergoes whiptail change, or hangs poisonous

like a cloud. At this point the organs are forsaken in favor of two electric guitars, the better to fashion a distinctive gestalt for each of these miniatures. Eventually the ball finds a pocket on the roulette wheel that's neither red nor black, green double zero

tells the guitarists to strum an atavistic sixteen bars of a C major chord atop the drummer's summoning of his first backbeat. No more bets. How long until the audience breaks the silence? It will not. This first number concluded, one of the two guitarists approaches the mic, offers a song in prose

of a kind, sung in sentences, in-

sufficient information/gratuitous information

It's better they don't serve beer in glasses. The singer laughs off the impact, shakes like a dog exiting a bath. By the end of this snippet of song there's little indication that a full drink had been hurled. He's soaking, yes, the guitar a tad sticky, but the eyes of the audience betray not a thing

and certainly no one. Everyone blinked. The warmth of feeling

rekindles as the group resumes its peculiar stumbling forward motion, a musical digressiveness based on jumbling the proportions of songwriting recipes so that a bridge lengthens to an endless span, a series of verses atrophies to a single iteration, chorus shrinks to grunt. Three misshapen songs later there's another exploding liquid fist, the singer blindsided in the act of shaping the first word of a song. Not only the aim, but the timing—it would be something to write

a poem about. The group delivers what remains of the song in an instrumental version while the singer scans the audience for the perpetrator and intuits not the slightest change on the collective face of the audience. There is no collective

face, there really is not, just expectant eyes and ears, and a homogeneity that over time will become apparent to all. Two beers from the blue, and on they rumble. Audience, which side are you on?

Same group, different configuration

just a core duo with rail passes. The asymmetry

of a duo

.

Two travelers trying to get their footing

as two. The difficulty in aligning when best to

shoot shit

A photo from this tour shows the duo onstage with acoustic guitars and glasses with thick plastic frames, an overflow audience seated onstage also with matching eyewear, the same person

times thirty, this must have been planned. The tour is a daily commute, the hushed existence of intercity train travel—muffled dings, murmured announcements, and the rare thrill of a flat-out sprint to nail a transfer. Days and weeks pass in quiet conversation and book after forgotten book. Overhead luggage racks in train compartments are almost large enough for dreadnought acoustic guitar cases; the instrument can be made to keep from falling

on Viennese businessmen when expertly wedged between winter coats. Disapproving compartment mates usually thaw in time for a parting nod. Rail travel is to the minute and marks a futuristic phase beyond the sprinter van packed to the ceiling and a month of punk clubs. It speaks to a different mode of music making, photo of the Ramones taking the subway to CBGBs notwithstanding. Ditto for duo—does this even count as a group?—and putting into practice ideas of a flexible ensemble that expands and contracts around a core. Improvisation writ everywhere

not only on the musical clock. A guitar is a cistern

for feedback coming to your town. Somewhere there's a radio recording of the group that documents a restorative nap by one of the members because the music permits it, could even be said to encourage it. A range of freedoms through which to understand delimitation, and vice versa. One night the duo encounter a fellow traveler from years before who watches their backstage rehearsal with skepticism and decides to level with them: You can't be serious. What's serious what's finished

what's finished too soon

what's unfinished too soon

,

what's prepared

what's overprepared

what's insufficiently overprepared

what's polished

what's practiced, what's

practical versus practicable

why do we write in the studio and only

afterward on tour learn how to play these pieces

Next year duo rail travel becomes solo. Different

group this time because it's not a group—just a human sans sobriquet. Strange after these many years to realize a dream of touring unencumbered, and then what? Solo scanning of timetables, solo changing of trains, solo in the dressing room and solo back to the hotel, solo in the many small towns ripe for relocating, in which to picture oneself playing the eccentric transplant. So much overnight television, fighting sleep to savor an unfamiliar language, the huge suitcase stuffed with reading material until the resolve is found to abandon books in hotel rooms and backstages. Solo means one set of hands to sculpt the sound

to measure decay to heart's unrelieved content

to duet with echo in shadow sword-

play in halls that would be a nightmare for an ensemble of any size, the gig over before it's begun owing to acoustics in which one band approximates a battle of, all entrants sounding simultaneously. The solo performer lets it ring, lets it rebound, lets it die, plays it as it lays, as it reanimates, and revels in the opportunity to follow each statement however lacking in semantics all the way to its conclusion, a spill or spray of logic never to be reconstructed.

The logic is sound. Let it have been.

Politics at a distance registers poorly through the warp of newspapers in languages one ought by now to understand. Are they really going to impeach the president? Grittier details

of the farce are comprehended imperfectly in a dentist's waiting room in Les Gobelins. Flash back to an urgent thumbing of the dictionary in an effort to wring meaning from every word of the *Süddeutsche Zeitung*'s coverage of Anita Hill's testimony. Distracted and fearing

his inability to communicate with the necessary rapidity during a root canal, the musician takes flight with all manner of pantomimed apologies. Leaves the newspaper where he found it.

There's the challenge of recognizing a face grown older, grown differently from how one imagined and far from where it was last encountered. You take their word for it.

A promoter from ages prior in Zagreb reappears in the Netherlands; years before in the weeks leading up to the referendum for independence, weeks he found unbearably tense, he accepted an invitation from a band to escape for the weekend to Vienna

and in Vienna another group was passing through and invited him to ride with them to Frankfurt, and then another to Amsterdam, from there to London and Birmingham and a series of construction jobs, finally settling in Amsterdam in a drift of however many years beyond his weekend trip.

Well-meaning friends will do anything to keep a soul from venturing out alone on tour in the States, even if it means a two-week blind date of a traveling companion, especially if it's an opportunity for someone who has never been to the US to visit a new city each day. Let's experiment

says the traveler from Greece, let's eat only at locally owned restaurants. At noon between Atlanta and Knoxville the musician and the international visitor pull off the interstate for lunch. It's a small town: Walgreens with an empty parking lot at the first intersection, McDonald's catty-cornered, two or three gas stations, Wendy's, and farther down a strip mall with Subway and Taco Bell. Among these I'd suggest

The visitor says to return to the highway. Five miles later they pull off at the next exit. Identical overstates it, but the first business they see in the next town is a Walgreens with a nearly empty parking lot, followed by McDonald's, several gas stations, the same strip mall, and they circle back to the highway without a word. After another five miles, the next town. This time the order is switched, but otherwise same

horror movie shorn

of opening credits. They repeat the action

for the next hour. The uniformity of puzzle pieces

disturbs the musician, unfixes what he thought he knew of tiny

towns along the highway, the geography linking part

and whole. In the process their hunger's

sated, lunch over-

rated.

That evening's show in Knoxville ends at 2 a.m., and the musician springs for the rare, once-weekly motel because no one offers a couch or floor. When he was a teenager all-ages hardcore punk matinees were a revelation not only because of the occasion for kids to congregate and form bands—a week's notice is enough—and just as quickly break them up and hate on their high schools and affirmatively slay one another

but also because everyone was sprung from the gig at five o'clock in the afternoon. Those small armies of teens exited into the sunlight of a different city, the White Castle now a hub for organizing, all those blown minds encountering their town anew because we have hours

'til sunset, the day raw with potential. Two in the morning on Knoxville's East Jackson Avenue is a different story, crypt-quiet, a line of trash cans at curbside the only visible commitment to the future. The next night in Nashville the musician has been given a two-hour slot at a Music Row bar, and for the first time in his life he'll be playing for tips. Insert punch line.

This curious arrangement brings out a rare exoteric improved version of himself in which he takes care to connect with each person in this roomful of strangers. Most every audience however welcoming is a roomful of strangers; these folks were heretofore unaware of his existence

yet the unabashedly rambling stories with which he introduces songs and instrumental abstractions draw them into his orbit. They toss bills into the tip jar every fifteen minutes when the woman who runs the joint pops out from behind the bar, gives a holler, and waves the plastic jar above her head, berating the stingiest patrons. She's a potent one

to have on your side. Midway through the set the musician is distracted by the sight through the front window of the international visitor swapping T-shirts with an impressively chiseled toothless old man. The two-hour slot forces the musician to plumb nearly the entirety of his repertoire; he succeeds in finding paths through pieces he hadn't contemplated in years, and with fifteen minutes left on the clock it's a welcome distraction when a Garth Brooks doppelgänger in white tee and black cowboy hat announces he's newly engaged and offers a twenty-dollar tip to borrow the musician's guitar and play a number he's written for his fiancée. To the musician's relief, this troubadour carries a tune right nicely, the audience thinks he's a catch

and it's a serendipitous end to the set. The musician is all grins as he hugs his guest, wishes the couple well, and expresses gratitude to the audience for luring him out of his shell, for showing him the loveliest of evenings on a first visit to Nashville

when out from behind the bar comes the boss, pointing at her wristwatch and ordering the musician to get the hell back onstage. He thinks she's joking—he's played for close to two hours, no one could possibly want more—but there are ten minutes left in the slot, she's got drinks to sell, and he needs to get back up there until the next act is ready to start. He apologizes, plays a couple of tunes he hopes no one remembers having heard, but for the remainder of the evening things will not be the same between the two of them.

Lost in Detroit several nights later, wandering through a vacant lot of chest-high weeds, the international visitor's cell phone rings and a friend from Athens wants to know all about the US, all about its cities and the beautiful hotels where they're staying. Of course

I want the great wicked city

with which the tour invariably concludes, everyone who's ever picked up an instrument wants the great wicked city, that's why you agree to play on a Wednesday night in the venue beneath the venue below the original venue, the Old Office Space supplanted by the Haunted Mine Shaft as the smallest room on the lowermost level in a warren of unlikely spaces, all beat-matched to the DJ set heard through your feet. Artists tell us they like how intimate it is how relaxed. The musician and visitor have little chance of arriving in the metropolis in time for the scheduled sound check, so now's the chance for the musician to take the visitor up on his offer

to share the driving. It's been their only point of contention, that and the visitor's suggestion that they avoid interstates to see more of the country. They fill up the tank one last time, switch drivers, the musician drifts off

and after a spell of dreamless sleep wakes to find the car stopped at a red light on a rural two-lane road, cows massed on a hill beyond the roadside produce stand, the visitor radiant.

The first time the musician emerged from the Holland Tunnel fifteen years earlier, it was as one of five teenagers in a rental van primed for whatever wickedness, and they couldn't fathom the traffic on Canal Street. Exotic gridlock—they'd never seen anything like it. These five souls were down for life accelerated, at least for a few days, for life as accelerant, and instead they found themselves stuck in traffic, debating how it works

how can this city possibly function, what are the economics undergirding it when people are stuck in unmoving cars, green lights come and green lights go, the spectacle of the box blocked in one direction and then the next. After thirty long minutes a tall thin guy raced past on foot with two burly guys in pursuit—two Hardys chasing a Laurel—weaving in and out of traffic until they cornered him in a doorway, and with hundreds of people watching from their cars delivered one punch apiece and strutted away. Two mornings later the group discovered that someone had broken into the van. Who leaves a rental full of musical equipment unattended overnight? You want the great wicked

maybe not

maybe not that way.

No one rides shotgun on the disastrous solo trip in the States several weeks after 9/11. We might start to consider all of this a single tour as the traffic at the entrance to the Verrazzano Bridge stretches into the new century. Like all of New York's bridges the Verrazzano is now guarded by military personnel, and the musician notes signs forbidding trucks on the upper level. Stuck behind an unmoving yellow Ryder truck on the upper level, he mentally replays the video of the Ryder truck parked in front of the Murrah Federal Building in Oklahoma City, the words "yellow Ryder truck" bringing to mind surveillance footage of the explosion in frame-skipping black and white as the bridge sways

and traffic goes nowhere. What are the odds of making it to the show and what could possibly be the point of this? The Philly traffic cop the next morning looks up from writing a ticket to see the musician hustling down the street, quarters in hand. She tears the ticket in half, saying, Y'all going through a lot in New York City.

It's snowing on Monday night

in Sapporo. Let's consider this a single tour. It's a tour that sometimes takes you places where you strongly intuit there will not be a next time. This quality of simultaneous hello and goodbye contributes to a sense of counting down, another location visited and crossed off a list not necessarily of one's devising. Try to remember Sapporo

even as you've just arrived, because you'll be there once and only for twenty hours, the countdown already begun. There hadn't been snow on the ground when the plane landed, but shortly afterward it started coming down in the thickest of flakes and accumulating quickly. The movie set wasn't properly decorated and now everything needs to happen on the double. It's the cleanest snow on earth; one hopes it snows every Monday night in Sapporo. Places everyone

The musician can't figure out what he's doing in Sapporo, what sequence of events led to his being summoned. Or why on this wintery Monday night there's a sold-out audience at the Yamaha Music School. He paces the long corridor

outside the fourth-floor concert hall, more anxious than he would typically be because he doesn't know a soul within hundreds of miles and can't rely on momentum from previous visits, can't assume that anyone in the audience knows him as anything other than a minimally plausible

name and photograph. The context for the performance is unclear, best to approach it as a single encounter lasting sixty or seventy minutes and consisting of what meaning can be made in the room. Everything needs to happen in the room. He paces until the young man stationed behind a desk at the far end of the hall attracts his attention by leaping up and waving a telephone, enthusiastically signaling him to approach. He hails with the handset

for the duration of the musician's journey down the long corridor. With utmost politeness the receptionist addresses the musician by his full name, confirms that he's the artist who will be performing this evening, and when this is settled states in clear, confident English that for weeks he has been looking forward to the musician's visit. Unfortunately

his job is to answer the phone, and he'll have to wait until the musician's next visit to Sapporo to hear him in concert. Can't the receptionist ask a friend to fill in for him? That would not be possible, although he has so been looking forward to the musician's visit. He'll simply have to wait until the next time to see him perform. The musician recognizes the futility of further encouraging him to abandon his post, or of sharing his conviction that there will not be a next time in Sapporo.

The audience at the music school in Sapporo is reborn as the oldest inhabitants of a village in Marche ready for the annual celebration of its wine. There's no snow on the ground. Three dozen people—elderly women almost exclusively, a well-preserved gentleman or two—occupy the first three rows of rickety wooden chairs

awaiting the afternoon sound check in the town center, and they're still in the same seats when the show begins several hours later. There was an announcement of a concert, a free concert in the main square. Above all it's a gathering

whether the cause is the new Verdicchio wine or the Italian Communist Party or the fact of being on tour in a country where one can play a dozen gigs in a row under the night sky—this can ruin a musician for ever playing indoors again—with the exception of one evening of torrential rain and a scuttled gig in which the Sicilian tour manager asks if he should collect the guarantee, because he'd be happy to try.

The musician was unprepared to watch the two silhouettes, tour manager and local promoter, back and forth and going at it like mad in the pouring rain, an epic argument of stark shadow-puppet gestures with the occasional truce during which the tour manager delivers a progress update

then returns to the fray, who knows the specifics of what they're fighting about for such a length of time and over numerous rounds. In the end not only does the musician get paid but they wind up staying a night and a day at the promoter's home where over drinks his Artaudian man-servant makes a show of attaching an electrical nerve-stimulation device to the promoter's saggy torso, his skin rolling and crashing in wave-like spasms. The assistant prepares swordfish eggs and the musician is tutored

on how to praise the meal. Never prematurely compliment the main course; instead start at the beginning to acknowledge properly the many decisions that went into the meal's preparation. Begin with the hunt for ingredients at that morning's market. A good first question might be: How did you select these swordfish eggs?

Solo doesn't have to mean solo. The musician finds his way back to touring with others, and then to accepting invitations to share a stage, to participate in a spontaneous culminating set of the evening, and from there to one-off groupings

that recur with regularity. Sociality reasserts itself, the inevitability of the rebound obvious in retrospect. It results in collaborations with individuals from near the arctic circle or wherever else you wish to name, broad concentric rings

traveling outward from a long-ago splash. When he first picked up an instrument, the musician was limited to making barbed antisocial noise with people who lived within walking or bicycling distance. The orbit expands, the expansion accelerates leads to awakening disoriented

on a train alongside five musicians silently filling out monthly employment forms. It underwrites a week of attenuated winter daylight and evenings in which the musician is seated in front of the television, handed a glass full of a bracing clear alcohol, and lectured on the Olympic biathlon and cross-country skiing. Is it true that other Scandinavian countries are getting away with tricks for which their Swedish counterparts are penalized?

File under schooling, every bit of it

when you've been at it long enough that squalling energy music again becomes the task at hand, the difference being that full-bore squall is now a recognized genre, has progressed in evolutionary strands and been shunted into taxonomies by researchers trawling for informants. The musician's cooling process

spanned decades, an exceedingly long birth of the cool, and presented itself as the valid, ethical trajectory until under the influence of friends and co-conspirators he senses the possibility of a graceful slow boomerang, revisiting memories of a once-molten core, generator of dizzying surplus

infractions infra and ultra. File under schooling all the years of mad-dashing and breakneck hurtling toward the next gig just because. File under schooling a debate in an airport bar when connecting flights to Chicago have been canceled and one faction within the group wants to rent a car to outrun the snowstorm. See also: collective composition.

File under schooling various disaster gigs, the excess of optimism that sees a geographically dispersed group flying in from different parts of the country on the day of the show, three of the four participants arriving on time, the fourth hitting weather-related delay after delay, but in a small miracle

touching down in the destination city at the show's scheduled start time. Push it back as far as you can. It had seemed a bust, then tailwinds shifted to favor the traveler, more nail biting on the runway, and finally a sprint to the cab, pulling into the parking lot behind the venue sixty minutes after the start of the show, the musician ready to be the surge that changes everything. Within seconds of bursting through the back door directly onto the stage, suitcase and guitar in hand

it registers that the group is drunk, dispirited, close to surrender. From the audience's perspective the latecomer's arrival only compounds the evening's perplexities.

File under schooling another disaster gig in which the rhythm section's last-second chemical bump hastens diverging paths onstage, renders them extreme. For the length of the show the root cause is unknown to others in the band: a textbook problem in game theory. It's three in the morning

the end of the festival, the first song of the set when a comfortably mellow rest of the group notices that two members of the rhythm section are prisoners in their own stiffened bodies, fearful eyes

pleading beneath a rictus visage, muscles cranked beyond hope of musical fluidity. Can't get started, won't get finished—a set-long grinding of teeth and stripping of gears. Would that they could save themselves or a lifeline be thrown.

File under schooling being heckled during a gig way out on the plains—persistently dull, disappointing heckling. Learn how to tune your guitar, and so on. Strong premonition of a onetime visit: this is the rare show at the end of which the musician walks offstage and instead of reaching for a drink makes

a beeline for the itinerary, not Where are we next

but When do we get out of here, suddenly needing that information down to the minute and requiring it haste posthaste, Where are we and When do we. The musician commits the details of the departure to memory, quizzes himself, and still not reassured rifles around backstage until he can lay hands on the actual plane tickets, stroke the tokens that enable escape.

File under schooling

the challenge to let each

gig retain its proper weight and

proportion. Not to telescope. Not to

allow the many afternoons and evenings

to pile high or harden into monolith. The tele-

scope reversed as pointless compensatory distortion.

File under schooling strategies for clarity

and recoverability. Why are some images—the present parade—more readily at hand? There are occasions that one prepares for, attends to, consciously frames the mental snapshot, click. Remembers to press record. Then it's rolling, you're still rolling, it's rolling everywhere

around you, doesn't stop of its own volition.

Press pause to meditate on the straining of

the mechanism. Press stop in an act

of mercy. Press eject and

give us the

tape

.

The musician squints in the darkness of the former motion-capture lab, flips on the lights of what's now an under-utilized classroom or oversized storage space dominated by a scuffed white platform with a projection screen bolted on at a right angle. As a neutral backdrop it suffices for today's task. The wielder of the cell-phone camera guess-

timates the necessary ten-degree rotation between each photo—the sufficient redundancy—as she gradually circles the musician, overcompensating with an even forty images to create his 3-D avatar.

The musician trusts his artist friend on this one, hoping not to be made a complete fool, even as he's historically been game for artists' schemes, wondering what became of the footage of him strapped to a lie detector singing the Carter Family's "Death Is Only a Dream."

The large screen at the front of the stage contains the still image of a pattern of interlocking polygons whose volume is suggested by three shades of blue. The pattern announces "curtain," but the eye demands depth. Distortion in the pattern in the lower half of the image causes it to spread out before us as ground—as stage—and at an indeterminate distance

the pattern decisively curves upward as wall, as back wall and visible limit. The pattern toggles between flatness and depth, between curtain and stage, as ranks of polygons within the nominally still image flip this way and that. Four unhurried stick clicks set the tempo, and on the downbeat avatars of four musicians fade in

atop the polygons. An unseen live ensemble with drum kit and twinned electric guitars behind the screen loops a syncopated shuffle and buttonhook melody whose upward turn repeats a nagging question. The projected avatars swivel and groove. Don't look away.

The audience sees the avatars up close.

The audience sees the avatars at twice human scale.

The avatars impress as something not designed to be brought so close.

A virtual camera zooms in on the avatar quartet, cross-fades from one angle to the next, from full-group establishing shot to individual close-ups, from slow left-to-right pan to the overhead strafing of high-wire cameras at football games. The polygons pose riddles

and the avatars will not be rushed. They truck along at their own tempo, and before long they're as out of sync with the musical performance as lip-synching artists half a century ago on live television, pantomiming that concluded with performers unable to keep a straight face, swapping instruments, goofing, falling

all over themselves. The avatars betray no anxiety about whether their pantomime passes. They have no problem keeping straight faces, and it's hard to imagine them busting a virtual gut. Their gestures are attenuated, soft, serious. A little stoned. Their method is doctrinaire do-it-easy.

The avatar drummer gently flails without semblance of stick striking drum or cymbal. He paddles slowly and steadily, shadow-drumming with one hand gesturing toward a floor tom, the other aimed at a shallow rack tom, both sticks landing shy of their targets. The implements— not drumsticks exactly—resemble retractable metal pointers or snapped-off automobile antennas. The two guitarist avatars have mastered the feat of playing without straps—their instruments float. Occasionally one of them turns at an angle where the image glitches and for an instant the guitar becomes transparent. After a quarter of an hour

the musical composition's sequence of building blocks halts, and what's heard first as a marginally acceptable noise floor crescendos over a full minute until it suffuses the venue, dominates the proceedings. This single unbroken swell of white noise coincides with the raising of the screen and the reveal of four human musicians. They're flesh-and-blood small, human small

equipped with mundanities like guitar straps and drumsticks of proper thickness. Four clicks of the sticks precede the downbeat, and the avatars again fade in, this time rear-projected behind the live musicians. Twist though the humans might, nothing flickers nothing glitches, nothing goes poof. The composition begins again, its now-familiar contours a respite from spiraling white noise. The addition of an electric bass floods a region of frequencies previously carved out and held in reserve. No more

reveals. The avatars loom at the rear of the stage, doubling and dwarfing the musicians, puppet-puppeteer relationship unresolved, and the composition is played in its entirety a second time with eerie fidelity. The audience mulls the details of a story twice told

and at the close of the second quarter of an hour, the completion of the composition coincides with the disappearance of the projected image—both polygons and avatars. The illumination now consists of the pulsing once per second of seemingly arbitrary combinations of dozens of lights spread throughout the theater. Each tick of a silent clock registers its own intensity of multihued lightning, a summer storm's agnosticism.

What cements the category of musician is

the filing cabinet of live recordings

never listened to, at best one

hands them

off

allows them to become someone else's project should they desire it. The drawer full of cassettes, minidiscs, CD-RS, flash drives never to be auditioned, they wind up sealed in boxes, they could be tossed in the dumpster, for years these have been politely received by the musician

and with genuine thanks. They swim in the cabinet

above a sedimentary layer of lire, guilders, Belgian and French francs, Austrian schillings, Yugoslavian dinars commemorating the handsome miner with helmet and headlamp, taxi receipts from the previous century—Rechnung or Quittung?—and the lone ten-deutsche-mark bill stuck to the bottom of the drawer with thirty years of rust obscuring most everything save the expressiveness of Gauss's eyes. Try to account for the presence of a dozen stray photographs that form a thin second layer above the defunct currencies. The earliest of these shows a musician stretched out on the sidewalk—eyes closed, hands crossed in a casketlike pose, suppressing a giggle—in front of a venue whose logo is stenciled knee-high on the wall behind him. Where a monk in a matter of minutes

will request assistance with a translation. The next photo captures a hometown bookstore gig. Given years, a snapshot of the most informal, workaday evening counts as magic, extraordinary good fortune to have found this, future observers trying their damnedest to reconstruct what once passed as an agreeable Tuesday evening. What's missing is the audience

of fifteen. The photographer felt she was doing the musicians a favor by cropping the shot, gently suppressing evidence of the meager turnout, even as the fact of the small number in attendance—be honest, these were friends—renders the event more deliciously remote.

The category of musician is further defined by the ongoing recollection of images from earliest gigs. These persist in originary intensities retrieved year after year along a sliding scale of detail, episodes altered and sharpened in the process of overwriting.

Music bled out

at those first gigs is remembered through songs rehearsed into the ground, drilled nearly to death, the hand and finger memory proper to a radically narrow range of musical destinations responsible for a guitarist's postmortem fingering of a bar chord.

Pop music organizes itself

around countdowns. We count down

to the top.

Start with an unknowable number of concerts

minus one, minus one, always subtracting. Thirty years later

still contemplating the gesture of an absurdly loud opening band taunting a small audience clustered for their safety along the back wall of a tiny club: We have four more songs left in the set. Three more songs and then you'll be rid of us. Two more, we're almost done. And now one.

When the music grows

diffuse, when the style is

premised on self-interruption

when the contours aren't known

beforehand, when the music in retro-

spect is dimly available, when the decision

to frame the shot is lacking, when there's no will

to disengage the pause button, physical memory become

scant, when you have stories to remember you will remember them.

There's the memory technique that involves expanding the list of destinations, prioritizing playing where one hadn't previously set foot. But even the return visit can be the opportunity to question the presumed familiarity of a location, to be stimulated

by doubt. What does one recognize of these surroundings? Not much. Street names, the names of neighborhoods, half-lives unexpectedly short. Let's get lost

not in the beauty of those three words or the trumpet's exhortation but in witnessing performers age before our eyes. Tonight they've aged only an hour in our presence, but they want you to understand that they're not the same group that started the concert.

X leaves the building in a dream manifestation of

the irreversible, code for an irrecoverability

of which we can be grateful.

The band left the building by shedding members, growing participants, firming up a core, flying solo, making peace with noise, morphing into avatars; we will have endless time

for terminology. They long since ceased to answer the call of the group committed to weekly rehearsals in reeking shared spaces, no longer carting equipment down a gauntlet of rehearsal rooms right and left, eight ensembles shaking the hallway. Drop off the keys

and sign for the deposit. The band left the building after a single song, they left at the end of an hour, they left after three years of trying to make it work, trying to make the endeavor worth everyone's while after each member fanned out to a different time zone. They never ceased leaving. We touch down after long intervals sure enough it's snowing onstage, but no one is dressed

properly. Next time in Sapporo means next lifetime in Sapporo.

One concert after the next a vector against recapitulation, return to theme against journey in miniature. Counting

up or counting down, remember being told

when you have stories to tell, you will tell them.

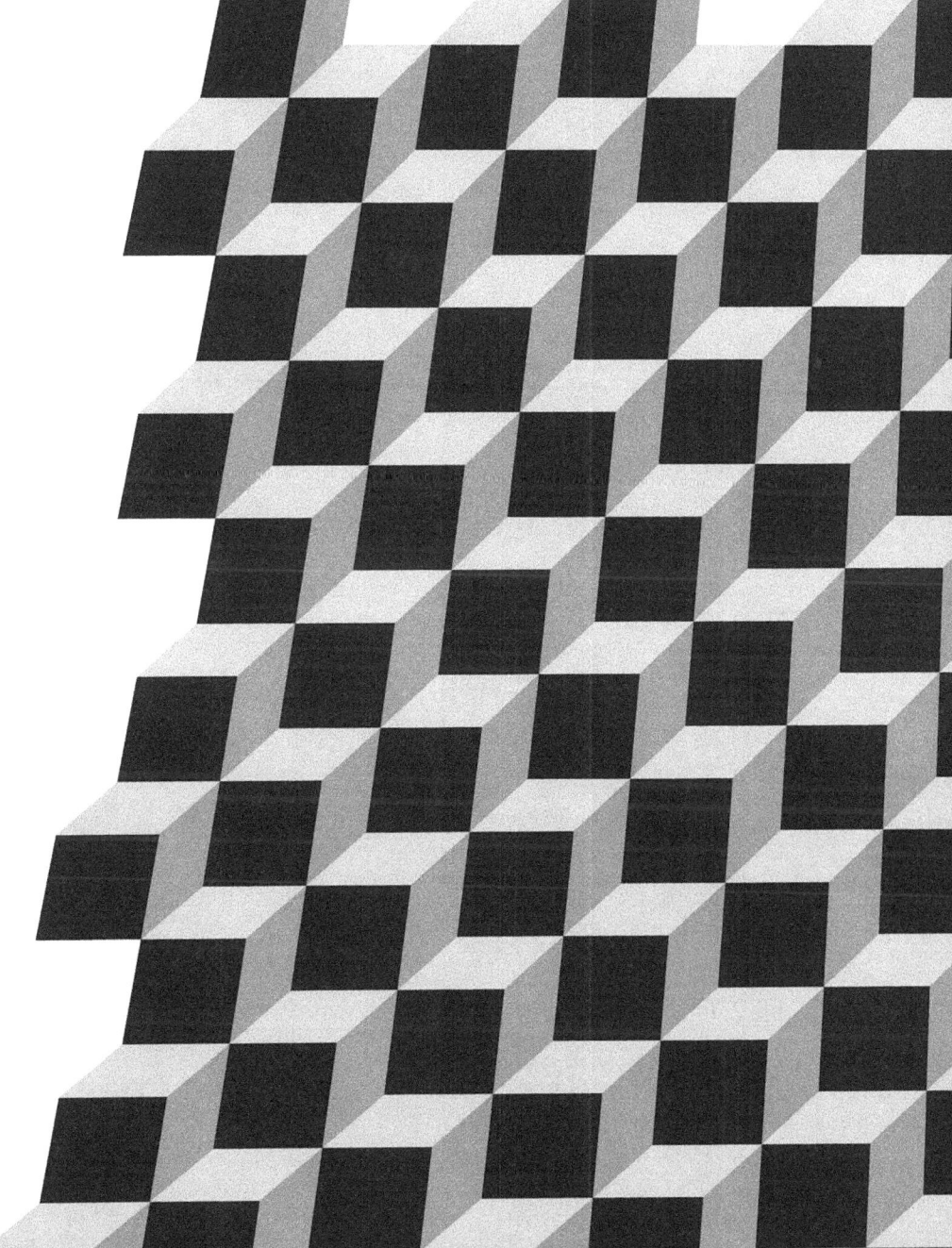

Afterword

Good night the pleasure was ours is the third and final entry in an ensemble of books that includes *Now that the audience is assembled* and *The Voice in the Headphones*. I'm inclined to describe these books as an ensemble rather than a series because there's no sequence in which they ought to be read. Whereas *Now that the audience is assembled* and *The Voice in the Headphones* are book-length poems that address single, sprawling days of musical activity, *Good night the pleasure was ours* by my reckoning spans three decades of such days. It describes the experience of performing music on tour, a string of daily dislocations that provides an education distinctly its own.

In its earliest episodes the unnamed musicians in *Good night the pleasure was ours* zigzag across a pre-internet landscape in which events of global significance are comprehended distantly and through translations from the people on whom these mostly monolingual travelers rely. These musicians have one job—to play that evening's gig—and the task resets daily. Much depends on whether a fax of a personal nature will be waiting at the next venue. The world outside the tour filters in with eccentric sparseness.

The various groups depicted here wax and wane in size. They move from being based in fundamental commonalities among members—a shared hometown, similarity of age, similarity of authorizing impulse that makes a group relevant in the first place—to skewing intergenerational and international, with a range of ideas about what constitutes a group. When I first imagined this book, I thought that its thirty-year arc might describe one long tour, with musicians, tour managers, booking agents, and the like in a continuous state of arrival and departure. In the end, it seemed preferable to include pauses for breath and regrouping, the better to represent different strategies for music making. What does it matter that this music is delivered away from home? We'd have to start with the significations of "home," a distant horizon in this book.

These three books emerge from what may seem like competing impulses—to open up music writing to greater experimentation, but also to engage in documentary practice. A student of Vito Acconci's told me that he once explained to a class that he migrated from poetry to art because art was big enough that you could stuff anything into it. Then he made a gesture of stuffing. I've had the sense while writing—stuffing—these books that everything can be made to fit, everything that wants to fit, and this comes from starting at a place in which music writing and poetry can be indistinguishable from one another.

As regards documentary practice, these books represent through close description three sites of musical experience:

the concert, the recording studio, and the tour. *Now that the audience is assembled* has its origins in dozens of concerts of experimental or improvised music for which I've been present either as an audience member or as a performer. (The monumental scene in Jacques Tati's film *Playtime* in which the Royal Garden restaurant is destroyed on its opening night also served as an inspiration, and for me registers as one ideal of art.) In a similar manner, *The Voice in the Headphones* might be said to take place in every recording studio in which I've worked, from a basement in Crestwood, Kentucky, to the BBC's Maida Vale complex. Initially I thought of that book as the opportunity to represent an impossible concatenation of spaces, a different species of studio encountered every time a door is opened or a threshold crossed. But as the fictional Skylight Recording gradually came into focus, it assumed a more coherent form than anticipated. The newly relevant topography in *The Voice in the Headphones* became that of the headspace of the musician working in the studio, especially upon hearing the talismanic words "You're rolling…" "Headspace" may seem as antiquated a term as a psychedelic wall hanging in a recording studio, but I haven't alighted on a more serviceable means of pinpointing the location where much of the drama—such as it is—of recording happens.

So many performances and recordings end where they began: same group. A competing aesthetic abhors a musical return and is structured around the desire that at the end—of the piece, of the album, of the concert, of the tour—the group won't be the same as at the beginning. Its members grew into different people, they split, they retired, they were unceremoniously replaced, touring took it out of them, they decided, "Enough."

Although work on *Good night the pleasure was ours* began before the pandemic, sitting in an apartment in New York through show after canceled show made the task of excavating sensations and impressions that best describe the privilege of playing music on tour that much more vertiginous.

Acknowledgments

The incantation "Don't leave me bewildered ... there's only one thing I can do, there's only one thing I can say" appears in the segue preceding the song "Lost Someone" on James Brown and the Famous Flames' *Live at the Apollo* LP (King Records, 1963).

"You want the great wicked city" is a phrase found near the conclusion of Susan Howe's *Souls of the Labadie Tract* (New York: New Directions, 2007). I think of Susan saying these words whenever the skyline of New York City appears in the distance.

Sincere thanks are due to the following people for the lessons of taking it on the road: Noël Akchoté, Andrea Belfi, Tim Blum, Cosima von Bonin, Bundy K. Brown, Angela Bulloch, Giovanna Cacciola, Tony Conrad, Drew Daniel, Kurt Erzi, Mats Gustafsson, Susan Howe, George Hurley, Steve Immerwahr, Clark Johnson, Rob Mazurek, John McEntire, Brian McMahan, Albert Oehlen, Will Oldham, Jim O'Rourke, Sooyoung Park, Stefano Pilia, Stephen Prina, Quentin Rollet, Atsushi Sasaki, M.C. Schmidt, Jan St. Werner, Mayo Thompson, Agostino Tilotta, Taku Unami, Britt Walford, Ryley Walker, Sabine Waltz, Tom Watson, Julian Weber, and many others.

I've found it a tremendous experience to work with the people at Duke University Press, especially Ken Wissoker, Liz Smith, Ryan Kendall, Nina Foster, Laura Sell, Matthew Tauch, Diane Grosse, Chad Royal, Jennifer Schaper, and Joshua Tranen. Excerpts from this book appeared in *Clip* and *Hotel*—thanks to editors Cole Highnam and Dominic Jaeckle—and as part of "Toggle Ensemble" in Angela Bulloch's *Euclid in Europe* (Berlin: Hatje Cantz, 2019).

Thank you to Josh Goldfein and Yvonne Brown for providing a place to write during the spring of 2020. Thanks to Cathy Bowman, Terri Kapsalis, John Corbett, and Ann Faurest for reading and responding to a draft of this book. John Corbett and Kate Pollasch at Corbett vs. Dempsey gallery helped in the search for permission to reproduce the Roger Brown painting that appears on this book's cover. Warmest thanks are due to the Roger Brown Study Collection at the School of the Art Institute of Chicago and its collection manager, James Connolly, as well as to my friend and collaborator Angela Bulloch for allowing me to include her images. Thanks to Delphine Le Gatt for permission to reproduce the performance photograph.

I'm grateful to the many people whose engagement with *Now that the audience is assembled* and *The Voice in the Headphones* helped me hone this book: Kara Bohnenstiel, Franklin Bruno, Craig Dworkin, Lawrence English, Luke Fowler, Sasha Frere-Jones, Dave Koenig, Wayne Koestenbaum, Lawrence Kumpf, Ben Lerner, Josiah McElheny, Daniel Muzyczuk, Benjamin Piekut, Ann Powers, Norbert Rodenkirchen,

Marina Rosenfeld, Cam Scott, John Sparagana, Benjamin Tausig, Charles Theonia, Mónica de la Torre, Eric Weisbard, Carl Wilson, and Amnon Wolman, among others. Special thanks to Andy Newman for a timely discovery in a rusty filing cabinet in his basement. And thank you, as ever, to William and Susan Grubbs and Ruth and Roger Bowman.

This book is dedicated, with love, to Cathy Bowman and Emmett Bowman-Grubbs.

Image Credits

FIGURE 1   Angela Bulloch, *Cube Pattern 12* from *Euclid in Europe*, 2019, digital image.

FIGURE 2   Angela Bulloch, *Cube Pattern Torqued 16* from *Euclid in Europe*, 2019, digital image.

FIGURE 3   Angela Bulloch and David Grubbs, *The Wired Salutation*, Centre Pompidou, Paris, 2013. Photograph © Delphine Le Gatt.

www.ingramcontent.com/pod-product-compliance
Lightning Source LLC
Chambersburg PA
CBHW062013180426
43199CB00035B/2639